Mess Monsters in the Garden

Beth Shoshan

Illustrated by
Piers Harper

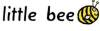

little bee

One day Mummy said
"The garden's a mess!"
And because it's so dirty
She suffers from stress.

I said,
"We need the dirt,
It's better – I know,
If it's tidy and clean
Then nothing will grow!"

But Mummy said "Nonsense!
That cannot be right!
I want nice paths and decking
And things to delight!"

What she didn't know
Was that locked in the shed
Was a big gang of monsters
From under my bed...

She'd told them to clear out,

skedaddle, skiddoo!

To stop messing my room up
As they used to do.

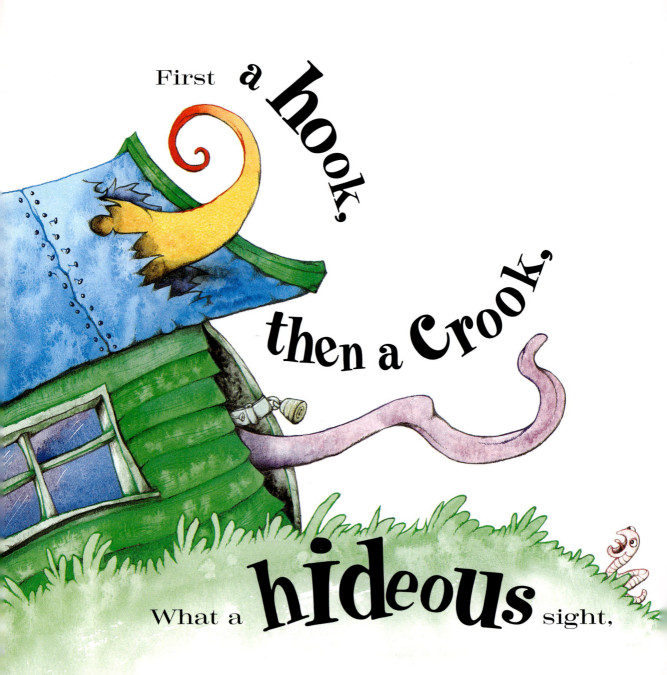

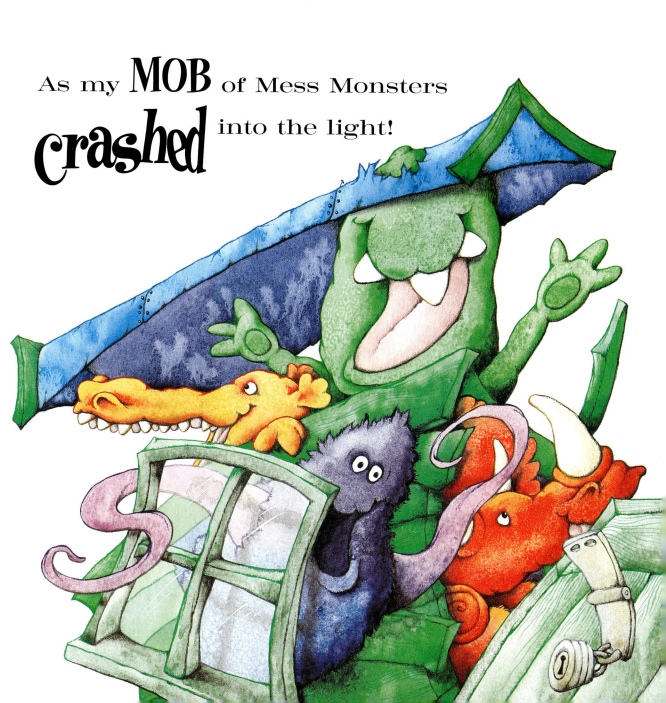

Those monsterous monsters burst up through the ground,

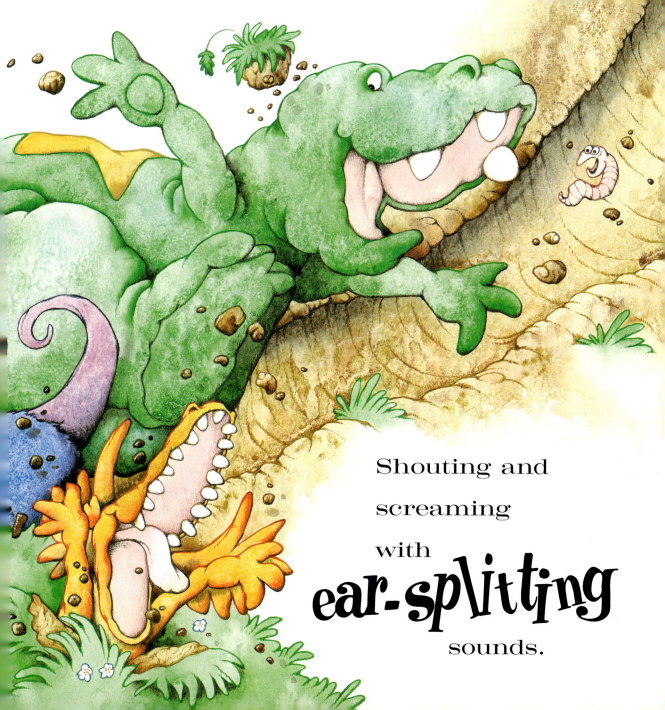

Shouting and screaming with **ear-splitting** sounds.

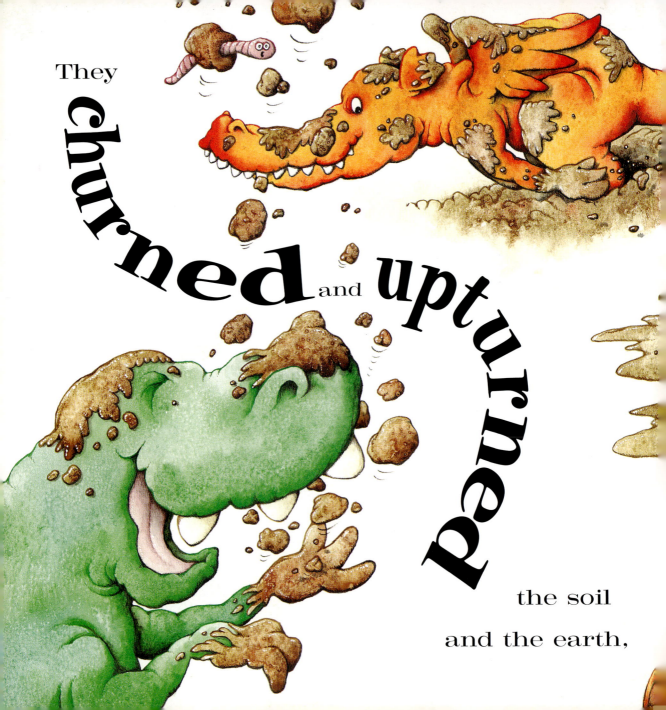

Throwing mud all about them for all it was worth.

Even Teddy was ready
To lend them a paw.
But they **trashed** him

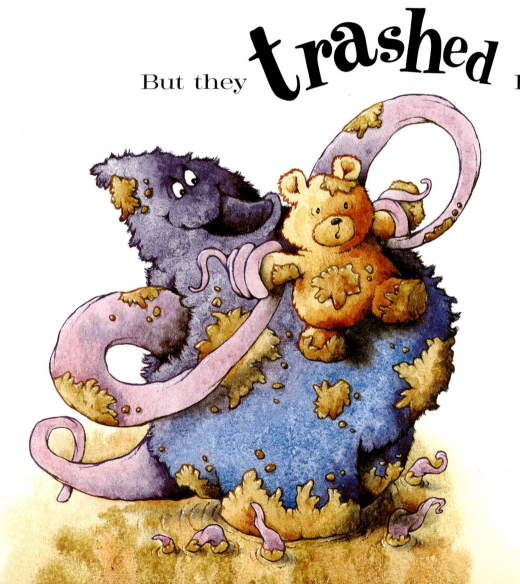

and **s**t**o**m**p**e**d** him,

And left him quite sore.

They dug up some toys
I was sure I had lost.
Then **crushed** them,

and **mashed** them,
Which made me quite cross.

I'd seen quite enough,
So I shouted,

Oi!

Stop!

And I handed a spade

To the monster on top...

So with bucket and fork
And a long garden hose,
Trying to avoid
any thorns in their toes,

They started to dig up
All over the place,
Throwing plants everywhere,
Getting mud in their face.

They scrabbled and scrambled
And worked through the night.

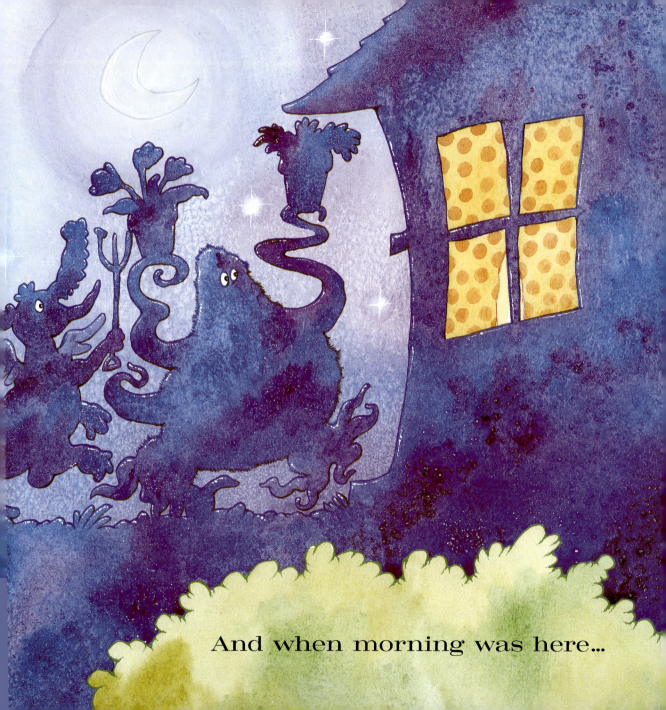
And when morning was here...

...what a fabulous sight!

Because...

Mummy was wrong

(Though we daren't tell her so!).

It's the mess in the garden

That makes gardens grow!

For
My Mummy
B.S.

For
Kate, Tim, Dan, Nick and Sadie
P.H.

First published in 2005
by Meadowside Children's Books
185 Fleet Street, London, EC4A 2HS.

This edition published in 2008
by Little Bee
an imprint of
Meadowside Children's Books

Text Beth Shoshan, 2005
Illustrations © Piers Harper, 2005

The right of Piers Harper to be identified
as the illustrator of this work has
been asserted by him in
accordance with the Copyright,
Designs and Patents Act, 1988

A CIP catalogue record for this book
is available from the British Library.
Printed in Indonesia